Traveling in Iceland: a native's advice on the practical stuff

Traveling in Iceland: a native's advice on the practical stuff

Birna Kjartanz

Copyright

Copyright © 2019 Birna Kjartanz

Cover art by: Þórir N. Kjartansson

Published by: BK Publications

~~~

In memory of those who have died during their travels in Iceland

Rest in Peace

~~~

Table of Contents

Introduction

The thought has occurred to me to name this guide "Driving in Iceland" since a large portion of it is dedicated to the topic. There is a ton of information out there about what to do in Iceland, how to be a tourist here, how to get where, the best hotels, restaurants, bars, all kinds of recreation, car rentals, entertainment, distractions and the list goes on and on. I will not write much about that but instead give you some insight into the culture, traffic, aurora photographing, a bit about traffic signs, driving in the weather here, information on what to do in case of emergencies, prepare you for unexpected situations you might encounter and more fun stuff.

I am a normal, 45-year-old, Icelandic woman with a full-time job, married to an American and we have one grown child. I worked in tourism for over 10 years and noticed some of the issues my customers ran into, that they weren't necessarily expecting when traveling here. I was born in South Iceland and grew up there until I was sixteen and moved away for school, sort of a preparation school for college, similar to senior high school in the United States. I also lived in the US for a year back in 1994, so I'm at least vaguely familiar with the culture there, and therefore maybe I can, with the help of my husband, predict some of the things that may come as a surprise to some Americans. At least some of the ones travelling from the DC or Michigan Area.

Every time I see a news article about someone who came all the way up here to have a relaxing tourist experience but ended up having an easily preventable accident – well, it just breaks my heart and I want to do my part in preventing things like that. I'm not a professional writer and English is not my native language, but I felt I should at least see how far my college English classes and my husband could get me. I love our tourists, who spent a lot of money and took time out of their busy schedules to visit us up here on this tiny little stamp in the Northern Atlantic Ocean. To me, it's still amazing anyone would even think of Iceland as a tourist destination. And I don't want to see people hurt when they're supposed to come here to have fun and enjoy nature. So, if this guide helps prevent even one death or injury, that would make this worth it.

Disclaimer:

This guide is for information purposes only and it is entirely up the reader if he or she takes the advice provided. I base the advice contained in this guide on my own personal experiences and perceptions as a native of Iceland, along with safety lectures over several years and decades by my father and other people who have experience in survival tactics in this country. My main audience is Americans since I'm more familiar with their culture than other ones, having lived there and being married to an American. For some reason, my writing depends a lot on me being able to compare this familiar culture as I describe my own. Hopefully, people from other countries won't be too upset with me because of this and can still use some of these tips.

Before your trip

I'm going to assume the reader has never been here before and isn't well versed in various survival methods, so expect the writing to reflect that.

In this chapter we cover the practical small stuff to think of before departure:

Clothing

Toiletries

Expect the unexpected small stuff

Clothing

As can be assumed from the name, Iceland is a country that can get quite cold. Not so much in temperature numbers but more in terms of rain and wind chill. Think the windy city of Chicago times ten, especially in the spring, fall and winter storms.[1] So, take warm clothes with you, preferably wool on the inside for winter hiking, skiing, snowmobiling and other winter sports. Otherwise, take warm clothing as if you were travelling to a Chicago-ishly, windy type of Colorado, albeit a bit warmer Colorado, if you will. Take plenty of socks and underwear if you don't plan on staying somewhere with access to a washing machine as laundromats are scarce and that includes Reykjavík. As far as I know, there is only one self-service laundromat, called The Laundromat Café, in Reykjavík. Bring sturdy swimwear if you plan on finding a hot spring in a remote area. No bikinis or speedos but a large, warm towel to dry off as soon as possible when you get out. If your head tends to get cold, bring a woolen hat to put over your wet hair. Always be aware of the hot springs that are too hot to bathe in. They can severely burn people and they're not always obviously marked if they are at all.

---

[1] I make this distinction because the fall storms are generally either dry, very windy and cold - or very wet, very windy and the windchill will make them feel very cold. Deadly cold if you're caught outside for a few hours. The winter storms can be either type of a fall storm in addition to snowy, blind, cold and deadly blizzards. Especially if you're travelling in the highlands, on the mountains or on the glaciers.

Do NOT swim in the ocean around South Iceland.[2] The black beaches aren't populated with sunbathing tourists for a reason and it is that the ocean currents close to the shore can get very strong and no human stands a chance getting out of the suction once in the water. The "suction" as I call it, tends to form because of the land shelf underwater being very close to the shoreline in some places so it can probably be compared (at times) to a drain pipe with strong suction. The ocean around here looks deceivingly beautiful and even peaceful at times. Don't let that fool you for one second, especially on the South coast near Vík, the place they sometimes call The Black Beach - in Icelandic it has always been referred to as "Reynisfjara" because it's next to the mountain "Reynisfjall". There have been some fatal accidents on this beach in recent years. Every single person who died was a tourist. So please heed the warning signs and don't go too close, not only if the weather is bad but also when the surface looks still and the weather is nice - the undercurrent is still there even if the surface current isn't, so there are sometimes tall and thick sort of "sneaker

---

[2] I'm not familiar enough with North Iceland so I'm only talking about the beaches on the South coast, ask the locals if you happen to travel up North.

waves" that appear as if out of thin air. I urge you to develop a healthy respect for the ocean around here - the locals were raised that way, whereas an American may never have even seen the ocean before and doesn't necessarily think to be careful (which is understandable).

Sometimes it can be really nice outside, even in the fall and winter time. You might need t-shirts and shorts in the summer time but very rarely in the fall and spring. If you're coming here to look at the northern lights[3] in the winter time or watch the fireworks on New Year's Eve in Reykjavík, make sure you bring something warm from toes and up. The cold seeps in everywhere because of the wind. I prefer Icelandic wool because it breathes without letting the wind seep in too much, plus it's water repellent because of the specific (and uniquely Icelandic) composition of it. A thick woolen sweater and a wind jacket, thermals underneath skiing pants, with a warm hat and gloves goes a long way on cold Aurora nights outside of Reykjavík. A pair of sturdy, water-repellent walking shoes or sneakers are a good idea if you plan on walking a lot. I have sometimes

---

[3] There is a short chapter on how to photograph those later on.

sprayed silicon on my sneakers if I know it's going to be rainy when I go hike on nearby mountains. Which reminds me, bring lots of disinfectant band-aids for foot sores if you plan on long(ish) hikes in the highlands or on mountains.

Toiletries

You don't need to pack too much of toiletries except your toothbrush and whatever medications[4] you may need. Over the counter stuff isn't readily available, there is no Tylenol or OTC melatonin and there's a serious lack of good OTC allergy pills. Same goes for anti-nausea pills and liquids. Bring an eye mask if you're travelling in the summer time since it's sometimes difficult to fall asleep during sunny(ish) midnights. It's always a good rule of thumb to expect minor accidents so bring a little first-aid bag with you with band-aids and disinfectants.

---

[4] Take a prescription paper with you in case the border police stops you. They are pretty strict on strong painkillers here for example.

It's probably best to find a Bónus[5] store and stock up on cheap toilet paper and trash bags. Always prepare for no recycling bins being around, until you happen to run into an open dumpster, especially outside of Reykjavík. If the dumpster is by a restaurant or another public building, it's just good manners to ask permission to dump the trash there since they're paying a lot of taxes on it. Back to the toilet paper. If you find yourself in the middle of nowhere and no toilets around, do your stuff but don't leave toilet paper anywhere. Any organic matter should be buried in the ground with rocks on top. As a side note – you have probably heard the stories of flying toilet paper everywhere and tourists going anywhere they stand. Those stories are (in my personal opinion) grossly exaggerated. If anything, our tourists more often than not, treat the environment better than the locals. But back to the topic. If you smoke, bring something to put the butts in like a half liter coke bottle with a little bit of water in the bottom. Then throw away with your other trash. Shampoos,

---

[5] Last time I checked that was still the cheapest grocery store you can find in this country. I always shop there myself. And no, I'm not getting any money for saying that.

soaps, disposable razors and stuff like that can be bought at Bónus.

You will find the hot water in the Reykjavík area smells funny, a little like rotten eggs. This is normal, the smell will not stick to your skin and it's not dangerous unless you're allergic to sulfur. If you are, do not shower in Reykjavík or any of the thermal towns around like Hveragerði without consulting your GP. Other towns have cleaned well/mountain water. Just ask the locals if their shower water is thermal or not. Most of them will know for sure. And don't let anyone tell you that you can't drink the cold tap water (that includes Reykjavík), you can and depending on where you are in the country it will be the best tasting drink you ever had. I'm very partial to Vík water myself :). Just be aware that you really don't need to buy water unless you just want to.

Expect the unexpected small stuff

Just a few things to keep in mind;

Get a location app for your phone in case you get lost.

Keep your personal information in an obvious place like your purse or wallet. Name, address, phone number of emergency contact, blood type, allergies and any information that could help emergency personnel if you're unconscious.

Check the weather forecast and road conditions on a regular basis and keep in mind that the weather and resulting conditions can change in an instant, especially during the winter. I will list some links later on in this guide.

Make sure your insurance and other relevant paperwork is in order before you come - it's expensive and time consuming for your relatives to transport your body if you have a fatal accident.

Don't worry about getting the Icelandic currency before you get here.[6] You can at Keflavík airport and any bank plus any ATM you come across. If you plan on going to downtown Reykjavík during office hours, remember to bring Icelandic coins for parking and public restrooms, which you will also need outside of Reykjavík, at least

---

[6] I'm not so sure banks abroad have the ISK since the 2008 recession.

in some of the bigger tourist places. There are also parking spaces that take credit cards, but the old-style ones are still common on the older streets in downtown Reykjavík.

Expect to get wet. All the time. Pack according to that fact. Umbrellas may not be practical because of the wind. It's much better to bring a good hat and even rubber boots and thick socks if you're just doing the normal tourist stuff like the Golden Circle and The Blue Lagoon.

If you plan on going to the highlands or any of the bigger mountains, make sure you always let someone know where you're going and when you plan on being back.[7] Check the weather forecast well before and also right before you leave. Don't take any chances and abort if you see dark green (a lot of rain/snow) and purple/pink (very windy) at the same time, on the weather site, in the mountain area you're going to!![8] If you run into trouble dial 112. They have location software to locate you and if they

_____

[7] https://safetravel.is offers tourists to register their travel plans online, I recommend using this option, especially if you're going to be traveling somewhere out in the middle of nowhere by yourself.

[8] https://en.vedur.is.

can't reach your phone, they can also access some sort of satellite service to locate you. But they will ask you where you are and other questions so you just try to be as specific as you can.

Most stores close early every day and most are closed on red holidays. There is one chain that has a few major stores open 24/7 in Reykjavík and the name is "Hagkaup".

You can not buy alcoholic beverages in grocery stores here. All alcohol (beer and wine too) is sold by the state in state run liquor stores and they also close early, even earlier than the grocery stores.[9] If you can buy your alcohol at the airport when you enter the country, you should because it's much cheaper. Same goes for cigarettes.

One of the things my husband talked about when he first moved here was size and selection in grocery stores. Everything seemed "smaller" to him. The milk cartons are just 1 liter compared to large containers in American grocery stores. Breakfast cereal boxes are smaller and most other

---

[9] For more information go to www.vinbudin.is/english/home.aspx.

things just seemed smaller portion-wise. Same goes for selection within brands.

Maybe it's also a good idea to download some kind of conversion software for lbs. vs. kg, liters vs. gallons etc. I remember it took my husband a few years to get comfortable with "thinking in metrics" so to speak.

Another thing to touch on is the wind gusts when on the road. Especially if you're driving here in the winter time, if the weather is acting volatile, you can expect strong jerky winds while driving past mountains and mountain ranges. It will feel like a strong jerk on the car, like something is physically pushing/pulling it in one direction or another. In other words, you will feel the car physically moving sometimes if the gusts are strong.

Don't pass the plow/salt trucks if you're here in the winter. They are there for a reason so just sit back and let them control your speed for a bit.

Street lights are on the side of the road instead of in the middle or above.

Ambulances and police cars have flashing blue lights only, not red/blue.

Chocolate/licorice candy really is good, and you should give it a chance :-)

Weather and driving

Like I've said before, the hallmark of Icelandic weather is not exactly the cold but the wind. If you think about Chicago and how windy it can be there, remember that it's located inland. Iceland is a small island close to the arctic circle. So, we have cold, Arctic ocean currents slamming into the warmer Gulf Stream flowing from the South, along with arctic winds mixed up with warmer southern winds above our heads. Greenland in the West with all its icy and cold greatness and the open ocean to the North, South and East. All that coupled with mountains everywhere and you get shifty winds with sometimes very sudden and strong wind gusts, sudden rain or snow and rocky temps. The most common wind direction here is from the East or South East. Something many bicyclists don't always think about when they plan their trip around the country heading East instead of North from Reykjavík. In any case, the conditions around Iceland create volatile weather conditions that might not be as common elsewhere. So, expect strong, jerky winds in the spring, fall and winter and to a much lesser extent in the summer time. One minute it can be completely still and all of a sudden there will be howling wind blowing by one second later. Often with rain, sleet or snow if you're hiking in the mountains. Another second later the sun comes out and you have to take your jacket off.

Don't make the mistake of thinking you're prepared, even if you come from a country with a lot of snow and cold. The location of this island makes it different from anything else you've experienced. Just don't underestimate the weather conditions is all I'm saying.

No one should plan a trip on a bicycle, in a camper or a motorhome in late fall and winter time, it's as simple as that and the locals generally don't do it either. There are sport bicyclists in Reykjavík who ride back and forth to work, but they have huge winter tires under their bikes and again, they're used to the weather and roads here. It's much more stable in the summer time so most experienced drivers/bicyclists should be fine during that time of year. The road system is nothing like the States though. Road signs are sparse and with only pictures as information so study the road signs before getting a rental car and don't blindly believe the GPS lady as she has been wrong numerous times before and lead unsuspecting tourists to unusual places. This happens more where it's rural. I think GPS coordinates should be accurate in Reykjavík and other bigger towns. I will explain the most important/cryptic road signs in another chapter. The roads themselves are very narrow and most roads around the country are one lane roads with traffic coming from the opposite direction. A lot of the time without any kind of fencing or security between the lanes. Keep your eyes on the tires of the oncoming car. There are a LOT of inexperienced tourists in traffic here, not only in the summer but the winter too. Please be careful and always keep your attention sharp. If you feel like you must look at the view, stop instead of taking your eyes off the (one-lane!!) road. It only takes a fraction of a second for you to fly off the road since the shoulder of the ring road tends to get narrower and narrower the further away from Reykjavík you get. The landscape around the ring road is sometimes covered with old lava rocks and I don't recommend landing face first on those (wear your seatbelts always!!!).

There are a lot of one-lane bridges around the country so memorize that sign well. One of the first things you'll notice is that traffic signs tend to be close to what they're pointing towards and you don't get a very timely warning like you're used to on US Interstates. The first car to get to a one-lane bridge is generally thought to have the right of way. If there's a line of cars, it's considered polite to let the line on the other end over if you're not too pressed for time, even if it should have been your turn too. Two or three cars at a time over a short one-lane bridge is normal. But if you rush on to the bridge, knowing there was someone closer on the other end, you might get the evil eye or a honking.

Be very careful when stopping the car on the side of the road to look at views or take pictures, especially in the dark out in the country. Both locals and tourists tend to drive way too fast for the conditions and darkness here. There was a tourist a few years back, who had an accident just like that. He probably came from a very densely populated country, and was just enjoying the silent, rural outdoors night in the middle of nowhere. But out of nowhere there came a car and sadly this tourist died. The thing is that out there, sounds are somehow muffled in a different way than in places where there are a lot of trees around.

Speaking of trees, with so few of them for reference, judging distances can be tricky. Objects seem closer than they actually are. Plus, the roads being somewhat wavy in the sense that they're on flat ground but there are subtle, wavy hills underneath, makes cars seem to appear out of nowhere. Remember that when you're trying to pass cars on these one-lane roads. Also watch the middle line (it's going to be white, not yellow). If the lines are broken but long, you might have these little wavy hills ahead I spoke about above. If the middle lines are short you should be OK but if the line is not broken, don't pass even if you see the locals doing it.

Beware of sheep and sometimes (escaped from captivity) horses on the side of the road. Especially in early summer and fall. The sheep go to the mountains in the spring and are starting to come back down in late August, early September. If you drive down a sheep and its lambs, you must pay the farmer directly and there might be a hefty fine on any damage to the rental car. Find the next farm you can see and let them know what happened, so they can figure out who the owner is.[10] If you decide to do

---

[10] Free-range sheep are marked with ear markings that farmers generally know or at the very least they can look up.

a hit and run, well…. just don't. You won't be arrested, and no one is going to beat you up over it. It's just best to keep an eye out for them when you're driving outside of Reykjavík. The eyes of sheep shine in the dark if they're looking into the light. The beam will create two, very distinct, yellowish to greenish circles in the distance when you're driving towards a sheep. If you see that, slow down and keep your eyes on the sheep the whole time you pass it. The lambs are especially unpredictable and can run in front of the car out of nowhere. If it's not dark, look for white blemishes in the green grass on the side of the road. There's a good chance it's a sheep with 2-3 lambs running around. And no, you're not allowed to hunt them down, kill them and eat them - even if they're roaming free, they are someone else's property.[11]

If you're planning on driving around here in the winter time it's best to get a rental with nailed tires. Four-wheel drive is always a plus, but the tires are the most important thing. Seventeen inches or more is good, a diesel will be best on gas and keep a tar remover with you in case you must get extra grip on the tires for some reason. But

---

[11] I read about two tourists who thought this was a good idea.

don't get too comfortable with all these precautions, it's still going to feel way different driving here than in the States. The snow here feels different driving in it. It's heavier and wetter, not the fluffy powdery type you're used to over there. The road material has a different feel as well, it feels rougher and noisy driving on it. You can certainly have a bad car accident even if you have a 4WD and nailed tires. Strong wind gusts to the side of the car and you're gone. Sudden black ice on the road, even with those nails and you slide right off or slam into the car in front of you. Always keep a decent distance between you and the next car. If the temperature outside is around 0°C, plus or minus 2 degrees[12] and the sky above is clear, always expect black ice. It can appear very suddenly. If the road is icy and those wind gusts are strong enough to catch the car, you're off the road in an instant.[13] The winds around the Eyjafjöll mountain range on the South

---

[12] This would translate into around 32°F.

[13] One of the things I check before I go driving longer distances out in the country is wind gusts going on at the moment (I do this more in the winter than the summer though). If they are above 30 and it's also raining or snowing I postpone until it dies down. I once drove on a clear road in 38 m/sek gusts and felt the car lift off the ground at one point. I was driving a 900 kg. Honda Civic with a wind spoiler circling the bottom. Note that I'm only talking about the gusts, not the average wind speed which can be much slower.

coast, Kjalarnes right North of Reykjavík and Hafnarfjall in the West can be especially dangerous in terms of wind gusts. All of the East Fjords can have very shifty wind speeds. Hold that wheel tight in those conditions and be ready for anything.

One other thing about the roads here you should be aware of when there is sleet or rain, is that the asphalt tends to have little "valleys" in them. They tend to "band-aid" the roads here in the summer with lousy road materials and so heavy trucks and nailed tires will do even more damage over one winter. So be very careful when driving those one-lane roads towards oncoming traffic in wet conditions. The jerking of the little but longish lakes that can form along the road can rip you right off and the car skips like a rock across a pond.

Always wear your seatbelts, don't talk on the phone while driving and never ever drive after drinking any alcohol. You really do need your whole attention span on the roads here. And the law is very strict, I believe the limit is now under 0.02%. Even one little beer and if you're caught the police will bust you for it.

Speeding is not a good idea in general. Aside from the fact that speeding on tiny, bad roads is never a good idea, the fines are steep. The speed limit is 90 km/h (55 m/h) but the police will leave you alone up to approximately 98 km/h. There are speeding cameras everywhere too and they are stricter. Personally, I just stick with 90-94 km/h. in the best possible conditions. Too many Icelanders are always in a hurry and the traffic culture (especially in Reykjavík) will reflect that but remember that they're used to the conditions here. They're not necessarily the best traffic role models is all I'm saying. And there are a lot of aggressive drivers around here, they will drive right on your a** with the high beams on just to "push you a little faster". It's those idiots that will make my blood boil but please try to just keep calm and keep an even speed until they decide it's time to pass you. In their defense though, because the roads are so narrow and hilly, sometimes it's necessary to come quite close before passing, just to be sure there is no car coming. You'll understand what I mean when you start driving here yourself. I remember my husband being shocked by this part of the traffic culture here, especially coming from the States where the traffic culture is way more sophisticated and most people keep a certain distance at all times.

Do NOT cross rivers in a rental car (or any car for that matter) under any circumstances. Ever, ever, ever! I don't care how well prepared the vehicle is that you're driving, you yourself are NOT experienced enough to drive across the rivers here. Leave that to the professionals. And any off-road driving in a rental is not covered by insurance anyway. If you MUST cross a river, you are stuck somewhere or in another type of danger, at least dial 112 and have a professional direct you somehow via the phone. People drown all the time in situations like these because they overestimate their driving skills in sneaky rivers. I would never attempt it myself even though I've been a passenger in cars crossing big rivers on several occasions.

The roads here are not made for bicycles so travel on those things at your own risk. If you plan on doing a trip like that, be prepared for angry and inconsiderate drivers who have no patience for bikes. And cars shooting by you so close to you that you feel the wind gust as they pass. And again, it's best for you guys to travel up North, to the East and from there back along the South coast, just because of the general wind direction from the East. It can't be much fun to struggle against constant winds and horizontal rain in your face. Side winds are strong, and the rain is horizontal, that's one of those "fun" facts about the weather here. Then there are all the large trucks that will pass you at speeds you wouldn't believe. So, a normal tourist should expect to get wet all the time, but a bicyclist should expect that times ten. And there are hills and mountains everywhere along the route. Narrow roads, very very narrow roads. Please bring a good helmet and a healthy dose of patience and strong nerves. Please just be extra careful when traveling on a bicycle.[14]

The traffic rules are a tad different. Here are the most confusing ones to the average American:

The dividing lines on the roads are white, not yellow.

You can NOT turn right on a red light.

If you don't see any signs or other indications on what to do and you're at a cross-road, the so-called "right-hand-rule" applies, ie. the car on your right hand has the right of way.

---

[14] For more information check this website out: https://cyclingiceland.is.

If you come across a dirt road only one rule applies, slow down! You don't want stones to rain over your car so don't do it to other cars. And drive like you would drive on ice, being prepared to use the steering wheel to correct yourself along with the clutch. If you choose a stick that is, otherwise take the foot off the gas. The same applies in the unlikely event you must drive through a cloud of volcanic ash which has formed into crystals on the road (this happens when it's raining), making the black ash feel like you're driving on regular ice.

Traffic circles are the single most effective speed bump one can find. And there are a lot of them in this country, especially around the Reykjavík area. If it's a one-lane circle you know what to do. But if it's a two-lane circle, remember that the inside circle ALWAYS has the right of way when exiting. So, if you plan on going straight, it's best to stick to the inner circle, use your signals to let the other drivers know what you're about to do, drive out of the circle (yes, cutting in front of the car in the outer lane, using the signal well beforehand) and like magic, they will stop for you. In the same sense, you must yield for inner circle traffic that wants to exit the circle. It's best not to change lanes once you're in, if you miss your exit, just calmly drive another round and exit on that second round. Keep calm, use your traffic signals well beforehand and watch other drivers and where they're looking, very closely.

Icelandic traffic signs - the most important (cryptic) ones explained

I once read a book by an American anthropologist named Edward Hall. He thought of national cultures in terms of high- or low context. High context meaning the general population communicates in a manner that relies on more than just words, like eye contact or not, touching or not, tone of voice etc., whereas low context is where information is clear and precise but non-verbal cues are minimal. You should think of Icelandic road signs as high context, wrapped in a supposed low context package. They are generally just pictures, without words and my husband said all of them seemed pretty cryptic to him when he first started driving here, even if America and Iceland have the most common ones in common. The reason, he said, is the lack of words to go along with these stick figures. I do remember driving in the DC area in '94 and how impressed I was with how easy it was to navigate such long distances and large towns/cities, thanks to clear markings and signs every 100 feet or so, using the road map I purchased at the local 7/11. It might be a good idea to have google translate handy when driving so the passenger (if you have one) can look up the Icelandic words they do put up on the road signs here. Anyway, I must limit myself to the ones I still find cryptic after having been an active driver here for the past 28 years as well as the ones my husband has specifically mentioned to me.

This one means there are crossroads ahead and the "right hand rule" applies:

This one means "traffic circle ahead":

This one means that the road is about to narrow from both sides, making it single-lane:

This one means there is an ascending hill ahead with a 10% tilt (there is another one in reverse that means there is a descending hill ahead with an x% tilt):

Speed bump ahead:

This one means icy conditions are common for however long ahead:

This one means high speed wind gusts are common for however long ahead:

This one means "other danger" or "be prepared for anything ahead". It is often used in combination with other types of traffic signs that should list something more informative:

One example would be this one that says "Beware - one-lane bridge ahead":

This one probably doesn't need words but it's an important one to look for in case of a natural disaster/bad accident in the area, so I'll include it. It means the road is closed in both directions:

This one means Do Not Enter:

Passing cars is forbidden when you see this one:

This one means there is no parking or waiting permitted:

This one means "end of all restrictions":

This one means "pass on the right":

This one lists the national speed limits pr. vehicle type in km/h and also directs us to have daytime running lights on at all times[15]:

This one means there is a toll booth ahead (Stans - Veggjald means Stop - road fee):

---

[15] Be sure to check if the car's lights are set to "auto" or not. The law here is that you have to have your lights on at all times, also in the daytime.

This one means there is a blind hill coming up (Blindhæð means Blind hill):

This is how they refer to a speed camera in this country (Löggæslumyndavél means Law enforcement camera):

This one means there might be a point of interest ahead:

This is a typical sign, listing distances (in kilometers) to towns ahead. What differs between Iceland and America is that the closest town is listed at the bottom of the list and the farthest one at the top. The framed numbers are the ID number of each road. The top one on this sign means it's 244 km to the town Höfn if you take road #1. If you take road #1 to Breiðdalsvík it will turn into road #96 and the total distance from where you are is 83 km:

This one means there is a single-lane bridge ahead, not to be confused with the sign that says the *road* is about to become single-lane:

This one means that the asphalt is ending and you're about to drive onto a gravel road:

Whenever you see a sign like this pay attention. The name of the road/area you're entering is "Hafnarfjall" in this case. The average wind speed is from the South-East at 27 m/sec., temperature is +6 degrees celcius and the fastest wind gust up to this point was 43 m/sec. If the "Vindhviður" (which is the Icelandic word for wind gusts) space on that signs is blank, then the wind gusts aren't anything to speak of and you probably won't feel the wind jerking the car around. I would not drive by Hafnarfjall in those conditions myself, but I probably would drive by the other place "Kjalarnes", just slower than usual. And I would have a firm grip on the wheel expecting those jerky gusts as described above:

Culture and the people

They say that Icelandic people are warm, welcoming and hospitable. I'd say that's true up to a certain point but in another way than the typical American might expect. The typical Icelander isn't openly friendly and chatty when you meet him for the first time. If you need help from a farmer for example, your best bet is to say something about the weather and then ask him something slightly personal like "do you keep cows or sheep" and "how harsh is it really to live here in the winter time" or "what is the most popular national dish you recommend". If you gradually get him talking, he will do everything he can for you and help you solve any problem you have if he can. Added plus if you make a little joke about Trump or something similar - people aren't shy talking about politics here and their sense of humor is, more often than not, based on politics. Other Icelanders (i.e. other than the typical farmer) are similar but there is always this sense of an invisible wall between you and them in everyday conversation. I notice this frequently when my husband is communicating with an Icelander who may or may not have a solid English foundation. Younger people in their twenties and thirties are a little easier to talk to though. But the further away from Reykjavík you get, the stiffer the English tends to get (not to generalize too much). If you're travelling here to see and experience nature, just stick with that and away from the people if you can. But if you're here to study the people and culture as well, then expect to have a little culture shock. You may have been told that Icelanders speak very good English. That's not entirely true. Most people can get by with English but to say that it's "good" generally speaking, is somewhat an overstatement.[16] Icelandic people tend to speak with a very harsh accent, and they say the sentences in English as they would say them in Icelandic with native punctuations and emphasis. Icelandic and English sentence structures don't mix very well, and so, this combination has a tendency to breed misunderstandings of sometimes gigantic proportions.[17] To you, as an American this

---

[16] I'm not implying my own English is perfect either.

[17] Just speaking as an Icelandic woman married to an American 😊

way of speaking may sound harsh and even offensive, but I hope you just take my word for it that it's rarely meant that way. In any case, sometimes you're going to have to get down to elementary grade English just to prevent a totally incomprehensible conversation that will leave you more confused than ever before. Ask simple, clear questions. Speak relatively slowly and clearly unless you're obviously talking to someone who is comfortable with English. Kids and elderly people will be harder to understand and talk to. So be prepared for misunderstandings and some language barriers.

The most common conversation subject would be the weather or (world) politics. A lot hinges on the weather forecast for us natives. Is it safe to drive to work tomorrow? Can the kids walk to school by themselves tomorrow or do I have to wake up earlier to drive them? Can the sheep stay out one more week before winter? All kinds of issues are directly linked with the weather so that's always a safe bet if you need to start a conversation or break an uncomfortable silence. The traditional Icelandic food is also an endless source of laughter and fun, at the expense of tourists and foreign residents of course. Just go along with it and you will be remembered as the "funny tourist" just because of your friendly curiosity. If you can stomach tasting some of it, go for it. Whale blubber, sheep testicles, sour shark and sheep heads are a common scare for the typical tourist. Very healthy and good for you, taste notwithstanding. Another possible conversation starter is the Santas and their mother. Many Icelanders are very proud of these old folk tales of "Grýla" and her sons, the thirteen Santa Clauses and their cannibalistic cat who prefers to munch on dirty children in old clothes.[18]

The typical Icelander doesn't understand sarcasm as presented by the typical American so don't even try unless you can sense it's someone who is used to American culture. Edward Hall, who I mentioned in previous chapters, considered American culture to be low context. Icelandic culture is the opposite in many ways (high context). In conversation people rely on nonverbal cues quite a bit, old sayings, tone of voice and eye contact to get their point across. I believe this is one of the reasons why Icelanders have a hard time getting sarcasm in spoken English. But if

---

[18] Yes, our parents really scared us with this stuff when we were children. No wonder we're *rumored* to be heavy drinkers!

you have a goofy sense of humor you might connect much better with them.

Americans, at least the ones I know, tend to avoid all talk about politics and religion. It's the opposite for Icelanders. If this makes you uncomfortable, the safest bet is to direct the talk towards the crash of 2008 and the so-called "kitchen utensils revolution" where people brought their pots, pans and banged on them with wooden/metal spoons in front of the national Parliament, every day for weeks. In any case, there are a few things Americans and Icelanders will probably never see eye to eye on when it comes to politics:

Trump - if you're a Trump supporter, don't even try explaining it. They won't listen, I promise you that, even if they themselves have probably voted for someone who promised a drastic change in this country. If you aren't, there's a good chance you will be able to have a decent conversation. If you find the person you're speaking with to be rude in a way you're not used to when talking politics, you could always say something like "well, I guess we have more in common than I thought, we voted Trump in and you voted the Independence Party in - again"[19]. This will shut them up every time in my experience.

The abortion debate - if you're a Christian of the "life begins at conception" variety, I'd stay out of this conversation. Most Icelandic women take their reproductive rights very seriously and most will guard them with a vengeance as well.

Capital punishment - I'd say the majority of people here are opposed to it unless it's a pedophile maybe. Iceland doesn't have Capital Punishment though just to avoid any misunderstandings.

Socialism - Icelanders and Americans view this concept very differently. Americans are told that Socialism equals Communism. Whatever your politics are, or whatever you were told about Socialism, it's not Communism. It's just not! Icelanders are taught that Socialism is a left-leaning, liberal concept first and foremost, where minorities have a voice and the tax burden is slightly higher on the rich than on the poor. There is solid social security, and no

---

[19] That's the biggest political party in Iceland on the right side of the political spectrum. They have been in power most of the time since 1944.

one should have to be homeless or go hungry. More importantly, we were warned that there is always that chance of Socialism turning into Communism with dictators and all that good stuff. National Socialism on the other hand, as in 1940's Germany, is thought to be quite different and right-wing. And that it has the potential to turn into right wing Fascism with dictators and all THAT good stuff. So, both left wing and right-wing politics can lead to dictatorship. So yeah, Americans and Icelanders define the term "Socialism" very differently in my experience.

Don't let seemingly rude and insensitive Icelanders ruin your trip, I can assure you they don't think they're being rude and would be mortified if they knew you thought that. Yes, you probably will think that at some point, even at several points during your trip. All I can say is they probably didn't mean it that way. If you keep Edward Hall's ideas in mind, the short and harsh-sounding Icelander who is seemingly speaking AT you, may subconsciously be using non-verbal cues along with that just like he or she would when communicating the same meaning in Icelandic. And probably never aware of how it sounds and looks to you as a foreign person.

The road less traveled

If you're here to discover places that don't have a lot of tourist traffic your best bet is to travel up North to the West Fjords (the North-western part of Iceland that looks like the "head" of the island). I've never been there myself, but friends and relatives talk about how beautiful it is. I guess there are quite a few dirt roads there and harsh weather conditions in the winter time, much harsher than here in the South. But apparently the scenery is just out of this world beautiful.

There are also cute little towns all over the island that aren't directly connected to The Ring Road with way less tourist traffic. Akranes is one in the West, Djúpivogur in the East is another, Þorlákshöfn, Eyrarbakki and Stokkseyri in the South - all of them beautiful towns right next to the ocean.

Þorlákshöfn has a very nice outside swimming pool with warm water. Which brings me to yet another cultural difference, Icelanders who see tourists going into swimming pools without bathing with soap first (yes, completely butt naked) might either give you an evil eye or even yell at you. Even if the pools have chlorine in them, being clean when you enter the water minimizes risk of various infections for everyone. So, wash well and let people around you see that you are indeed washing yourself well. Nobody dwells on naked people in the showers in those swimming pools so leave all prudish thinking like that on the airplane. Your naked body is just like ours, we've all seen each other naked before, it's really not that serious, trust me :). But I digress, walking around Þorlákshöfn, on the black beach and around the rocky shores is simply breathtaking. And there's even a decent golf course almost right there on the beach. Black Beach Tours is a small tourist company that provides unconventional entertainment like yoga sessions on the beach if weather permits and fishing/yacht tours.[20] If you feel like getting a little seasick for a few hours, there might be a ferry going to the Westman Islands soon, be sure to check with the locals where to get schedules. There are three family-owned, nice looking restaurants in

---

[20] https://blackbeachtours.is

Þorlákshöfn with good food and decent pricing (Iceland is expensive for tourists though, depending on the strength/weakness of the ISK against other currencies like the USD or the EUR).

Eyrarbakki, Stokkseyri and Akranes are also quiet little ocean towns/villages with small restaurants that have very good seafood. You should really try the small restaurants around these towns. Many of them have fresh seafood that almost melts in your mouth (I personally recommend the Icelandic lobster - it tastes a little sweeter than lobster elsewhere).

I'm not very familiar with Djúpivogur but it sits on a beautiful spot by the ocean with amazing views over the fjord it's located at. Really all the little towns in the East Fjords have these very cool views but be careful driving on the roads there. They're narrow and sometimes go along very steep mountain slopes, some of them on barely passable dirt roads. If you're driving around there in the spring time, be on the look-out for mud/rock slides and avalanches in the winter time. I'm a little nervous driving there myself during that time of year but the locals are rock stars who fear nothing when driving.

One of my all-time favorite places to visit is a little mountain called Hjörleifshöfði[21], not very tall, which sits on a vast black sand desert called "Mýrdalssandur" just East of Vík. It's said that the second settler of Iceland, who was also the foster brother of Leif Eiriksson, settled at Hjörleifshöfði when the two men sailed up here on their Viking ships back in the day. According to legend, Hjörleifur's slaves (who he kidnapped in Ireland before coming here, real nice guy obviously) killed him and it's said that he's buried at the top. There was some farming on the mountain until the 1918 Katla eruption so there are ruins there that are very interesting to see. This used to be a legit old-style farm made of stone, dirt and grass. The farmers had their cows in the basement and slept above them on the second floor because of the warmth they provided in the cold, harsh winters.[22]

There is fresh water (the best and cleanest water I have ever tasted in my life, no joke!) in a little stream at the foot of this mountain, a little further to the southern tip

---

[21] Sadly, it's for sale right now so it may get closed for tourist traffic in the near future, depending on who buys it. I would buy it myself but unfortunately, it's *somewhat* out of my price range.

[22] Halla Kjartansdóttir. (1995).

of it, close to where the walking path up to the ruins starts - don't hesitate to fill your water bottles with as much as you can carry with you. Walking up to the ruins is an easy hike for most people. People in bad shape might have to stop quite often to catch their breath but it only takes about 10 minutes to walk up there. If the plan is to go all the way up to see the burial ground, that takes longer, and the hills up are steeper so be careful not to fall and hurt yourself. And if you want to live dangerously, in the rock straight South of the old farm[23], at the bottom of the cliff, there is a track straight up the rocks with supporting lines in some places - this track leads right up to the ruins. It's a short climb but steep. Just note that there are no warning signs to speak of around there so do all of this at your own risk and evaluate your physical shape and your hiking gear first. It's probably rather humiliating to call 112 to be rescued from a cliff like that because you're too scared to go back down. But it happens quite often to people, not just tourists, so just try to stay safe. If you get to the top where the burial ground is, be sure to sign the guestbook that's always there in the summer time. If

---

[23] Be careful when you approach from up there. There have been a couple of accidents where people fall off the cliff.

you're alone or not in a large group and the weather is still, just lay down, close your eyes and really take in the sounds of nature and the ocean for a minute. There is no silence like that kind of "nature" silence as I refer to it in my own mind. All I need is 10 minutes up there in complete silence and my batteries are charged again.

Other quiet and beautiful places that I've heard of and seen pictures from but haven't been to myself (but plan to) include:

Hornstrandir Nature Reserve in the West Fjords.

Drangsnes, a pretty little village in the West Fjords.

Grímsey, an island North of where Húsavík is located.

Húsavík, a town not connected to The Ring Road, there is whale watching there.

Snæfellsjökull National Park. There might be some tourist traffic, but it shouldn't be too much and it's a large area too.

Lakagígar - the line of craters that opened up in the year 1783. Google "Skaftáreldar eruption" or "Laki" for more detailed information.

Fjallabak. This isn't exactly a place but rather a route up in the highlands North of the Mýrdalsjökull glacier. I've been told there's a hidden hot spring somewhere along that route. Be sure to have the right kind of car and gear if you plan on going there along with all the other safety precautions referred to above.

Langisjór - a large and long lake up in the highlands by the South-Western side of Vatnajökull glacier.

Gæsavatn - this is a beautiful, heart shaped lake North of Vík, up towards Mýrdalsjökull glacier.

A few tips about the northern lights

Many people are interested in the northern lights (or Aurora Borealis) and in taking pictures of them. They can only be seen during the fall and winter months when it starts getting dark again. I'm no expert on this breathtaking phenomenon but here is a step-by-step description of what you may need to get, not just to take OK pictures, but really cool ones:

Useful information regarding viewing of Aurora Borealis

Between the middle of August or so, until the middle of April, the Icelandic night is starting to be sufficiently dark to view Aurora Borealis. Clear skies are a must for this. The Icelandic Weather Service's cloud prediction can be very useful:

http://www.vedur.is/vedur/spar/skyjahula

However, even though the skies are clear, this is not a guarantee for seeing Aurora Borealis. That depends on solar flares and

Aurora predictions can be rather inaccurate. There are web-sites which show Aurora in real-time, they can be very helpful:

http://www.aurora-service.eu/aurora-forecast
http://www.swpc.noaa.gov/pmap
http://www.raunvis.hi.is/~halo/leirvogur.html

There is no rule as to when or for how long Aurora can be seen during the night. Therefore, it is necessary to be constantly prepared and, on the look-out as the lights can appear as suddenly as they disappear. It is best to be outside city/village lights which affect our ability to see the lights. It varies a lot how bright the lights are, how colorful and how much they move around. During a half or a full moon, they often seem less bright because of the moonlight but the upside is that, for those taking pictures, that the forefront of the pictures is better lit.

Instructions for Aurora Borealis photography

A camera tripod is a must and it's best to use as bright as possible (F/2,8 or more) and as wide a lens as possible. Have the settings on manual. Focus also set to manual and "infinity". Take the picture in RAW format to achieve the best results and to be able to change the white balance afterwards. For those who don't have these options it's best to set the camera to a rather "cold" white balance. It's usually best to film in as short as the equipment offers, so that the lights don't get mixed together if fluctuating fast across the sky. ISO 800-1600 is good if your camera can handle that without the picture turning grainy. Set the lens to its maximum aperture. Light the picture for 5-10 seconds and then observe if it's correctly lit. Then change the time and/or ISO depending on if the picture needs to be darkened or brightened. The Aurora can change their brightness very fast so it's necessary to stay alert to the outcome if that happens. It's hard to fix "burned" Aurora in any picture programs.

With hope that the above could be of help to you. Have fun![24]

---

[24] Þórir Kjartansson. (2018).

In case the impossible happens and what to do about it

Hopefully your vacation will just be a pleasant experience with no unexpected and potentially dangerous situations coming up. Most likely it will be. But like the guys on Monty Python used to say: "Nobody expects the Spanish Inquisition". You should develop this philosophy during your travels here and expect the unexpected. Here are a few real-life examples of situations where tourists and locals alike were severely injured or even died. Having said that, I need to stress that the likelihood of you having problems like these are minimal, you're probably more likely to have a car crash on the way to the airport than this. But it's better to be prepared in the unlikely event something bad happens, so here goes.

There are three rules to follow and these apply to all the situations described below:

- Above all, your first order of business is to keep warm for as long as possible.
- Stay calm and take slow deep breaths, in through your nose and out through your mouth, so you don't panic.
- Stay where you are unless you're in immediate physical danger.

You're stuck in a snowbank on a mountain road and can't move the car at all. What do you do?

If the weather is decent and you're not in danger of hypothermia or in another type of danger, the only way is to call the tow truck service (see next chapter with phone numbers) if you don't have anyone with you to push the car. If you want to try to get it out yourself first, just be careful not to damage it. If the car doesn't move at all you're going to need to dig the snow away from the tires. If you have something that could create some resistance for the tires, like a thin wooden plank or something similar, use that along with the tar remover spray for the tires, you bought at the gas station. Put the plank down on the ground where the tires are to try to have them "grab" it to inch the car out. Rocking it slowly back and forth, using the stick if it's a stick shift, without the tires spinning (spinning them fast just gets you more stuck) often works but may take some time so be patient. Other than that, you could try waving down a car that is likely to have rope and the ability to pull you out. If there's a farm nearby you should walk there if it's safe and see if they're willing to help out with a tractor. Most farmers would and do all the time, even in the middle of the night.

If you're on a road where there is more traffic it's best to stay inside the car and put on the hazards. Before you settle down for a long wait, make sure the exhaust pipe isn't clogged up with snow. We wouldn't want the fumes in the car while you're waiting. Then call the tow truck service and relax. If there are more cars around you, also stuck, the rescue squad people are probably on their way so you may not need the tow truck service after all. Unless someone stops to help which is more than likely. Many Icelandic men on trucks love this kind of stuff. One thing to keep in mind; I have *heard* that car insurance on rental cars doesn't cover damage made by other people than the person renting the car. So, the rescue squad or said truck drivers might be hesitant because of that. Don't take my word for it though and ask the car rental service person.

You went to the Black Beach in South Iceland, went too close to the water and a wave caught you and threw you out to sea. What do you do?

Ocean temps around Iceland are between 8°C and 10°C in the summer and 2°C and 3°C in the winter so you will get cold very quickly and weak as a result along with difficulty concentrating. I was always told that on average, hypothermia sets in within an hour in water below 5°C but it takes quite a bit longer in 10°C water, or up to two hours. But the temperature isn't your only problem, it's also the strong ocean currents and waves all around you throwing you around like a ragdoll. As always, it's important not to panic if possible since that accelerates your heart rate and wastes your energy and the little warmth you have left in your body. Breathe slowly in through your nose and out through your mouth to prevent swallowing ocean water and to calm down.

Get rid of your shoes or clothing only if you feel like they're sinking you, otherwise keep them on as they might help keep you afloat and protect your skin from the cold. Try to let yourself float on your back and try to "ride the waves" without having your arms too far away from your body (you'll lose warmth quicker that way). Think of the waves as an oversized 80's waterbed with very cold water and a lot of waves. If you have anything to hold onto, use it. Also try to keep your lungs half full of air without swallowing ocean water (they will act as little air tanks to keep you afloat). If you're close to the rocky shore with a lot of crashing waves against those rocks, be very careful when trying to reach them. Many people don't die from drowning but from being knocked around by waves and slammed into the rock. And with your weakened state, you're in severe physical danger. It's a bit of a Sophie's choice to choose between swimming to a shore with crashing waves against dangerous rocks and staying where you are trying to stay alive until you get help or finding another way out. I guess going with your gut on that one is the best bet.

You didn't take my advice, tried to cross a river yourself and now you're stuck in the middle of it with water coming up higher and higher, plus you feel the car starting to slide with the current. What do you do?

If you have an open window, get out as soon as possible but don't try to swim ashore if the current is strong and the river is large. Many of the larger rivers seem calm on the surface but have strong currents and rocks everywhere along the way. So, it's best to stay by the car or on the car for as long as possible. The rocks might knock you out and the currents might grab you, so you float helplessly down that river until it decides it's time for you stop. Locals and tourists alike have died trying to swim ashore in these situations. So, it's safest to climb on top of the car and wait there for help if it sits relatively stable in the river.

If your windows weren't down when the car got stuck and you can't open a door or a window because of pressure from the outside, keep calm and wait for the water to fill the car. Once the pressure is the same inside the car as it is on the outside, you should be able to get the window down or open a door. When you exit the car, look around first and try to avoid any rocks in sight because the current might grab you if you can't hold on to the car. Get to the surface to get some air and try to stabilize yourself using the car somehow, until help arrives. Not giving into the current and letting go of the car is the most important thing for now. But also keep in mind that the water in the rivers can be very cold, even colder than the ocean.

A volcanic eruption is in progress close by. What do you do?

If it's an eruption underneath a glacier like the 2010 Eyjafjallajökull eruption, there will not be lava so don't worry about that. What you DO have to worry about is flooding, ashfall and lightning inside that ashfall. The most notable volcanoes of that sort, that are close to people are Katla which is located in the Mýrdalsjökull glacier, just North of Vík in the South. And also, Öræfajökull glacier which is in the southern part of Vatnajökull glacier. Both volcanoes are very dangerous and potential flood paths from them are over The Ring Road in those areas, so heed all warnings and directions of rescue squad personnel. I believe there is a warning system connected to the phone system in case of these volcanoes erupting. So, if your phone is connected through a roaming service or you have a cheap Icelandic cellphone with a temporary Icelandic number, you will get the warning texts in English - do what those texts tell you to do. They have been preparing and planning for these volcanoes to erupt for decades.

In case of flooding the important thing to do, if you're stuck in the flood path is to get to higher ground immediately and seek any kind of shelter from the ashfall. Depending on the rock composition in the volcano, the ashfall can be quite toxic and heavy on your lungs, especially if you have asthma or other similar problems. However, it's thought that Katla's ashfall isn't as bad as the ashfall from Eyjafjallajökull. If you have your car as a shelter, close the airducts so there is no air coming into the car from outside. Just open the car door slightly for a minute to let in new air if you feel like you're running out of it (maybe putting up a towel first to prevent the ash from seeping in as you open the door). Being caught outside in the total blackness of volcanic ashfall is bad and you must seek any kind of shelter you can find right away. And cover your nose and mouth with anything you can find if you don't have a dust mask around.

Anyway, the car is actually ideal in case there is lightning activity because of the rubber tires under it. If you're caught in the middle of either one of the black deserts around those two volcanoes (for example in the desert around Hjörleifshöfði) get out of there, right now. From what I've read about Katla, from the time the glacier is breached until the melted ice in the form of a flood reaches The Ring Road on Mýrdalssandur, it takes anywhere from thirty minutes up to an hour. Even shorter when it comes to Öræfajökull because its slopes are way steeper and much higher so the speed of the flood will also be faster. I have heard people talk about 20 minutes which is not a long time to escape.

If it's a lava eruption there is also ashfall but the most dangerous situation you can run into is to be stuck in the path of the lava. You're pretty much toast (pun intended) if that happens so there's not much to say about that except lava flow tends to travel faster, the younger the eruption is and the closer to the source it is. The farther away the lava gets from the crater, the more it slows down. If the only way to run is towards water, try to stay afloat on top of something as the mixture of lava and salty ocean water quickly becomes acidic. The Sulphur pollution from lava eruptions can be very sneaky and dangerous so be aware if the "egg smell" gets very strong and you start getting a headache. If that happens, chances are great that you're standing or sitting in the middle of some sort of small valley. Get out immediately as Sulphur tends to sit closer to the ground. That said, you may smell sulfur sometimes when passing geothermal plants or glacier rivers. That's normal and not dangerous for you.

You're climbing steep, rocky slopes of a mountain and you realize you can't get back down. What do you do?

If you're feeling scared to the point of panic, don't move an inch unless it's to make sure you're not going to be blown away by wind gusts. You're way more likely to fall if you're in panic mode. Get your head cleared and focus on the issue at hand. Make sure you're in a good spot where you're shielded from rain, cold and wind and you're not in immediate danger of falling. Then call 112. If you're not sure where you are, they might be able to pinpoint your location with GPS via your cellphone or a satellite service. Just work with 112 as well as you can and answer all their questions to help them find you. Usually, when people injure themselves during mountain hikes or become stuck, the rescue squad first evaluates the weather to see if they can have the helicopter pick you up. Otherwise there will be a team sent on foot to you with a stretcher if you're hurt. We are rather proud of our rescue squad members in this country, similar to the pride Americans feel for their firemen. These are normal guys and girls who are volunteers, have day jobs, families and a normal life like the rest of us, but have a passion for all things survival- and wilderness related, plus they are highly trained. They get a lot of leeway at their jobs because of their membership in the rescue squads. There is a silent agreement between Icelandic employers that those people can be called out on a mission away from their jobs, with very little notice at any given time. They have all gone through extensive training and tend to be in top physical shape as well. So, you can trust them to rescue you if you were ever in doubt.

You went on a glacier hike or a glacier snowmobile trip and got separated from the group and there's a storm hitting. What do you do?

Hopefully you have already invested in Icelandic woolens and are wearing them closest to your skin from head to toe. That really does go a long way in keeping you warm and dry for as long as possible until you get help. Yes, it feels stingy to some people but there are also softer wool types around like angora wool, which is composed mostly of lamb's wool along with the angora. That's also OK as well as the so-called boiled wool, made in Norway - that wool type doesn't sting me at all and is very warm and cozy. Merino wool and Alpaca are also quality woolens. I prefer Icelandic wool simply because it's the only clothing that has kept me consistently warm over the years, living here. I don't like fleece for instance. It's really nothing more than soft plastic. And you know what happens if plastic catches on fire next to your skin. No such thing with Icelandic wool. It's quite expensive but it will keep you warm.

So, you're well dressed and have some water with you, maybe even a bar of dark chocolate. First thing, as usual, is to not give into panic. Take a few deep breaths and try to calm down because you need a clear head and your energy more than ever. If this is the type of blizzard where you can barely see the hands in front of you it's imperative to stay where you are, close to the snowmobile (if that's the type of trip you're on). If you're on a glacier it's even more important to stay put because it's probably littered with snow-covered and constantly moving crevasses. So, keeping calm, warm and staying where you are is your job now. If there is enough snow, dig yourself into it or try to shovel it over you to get shelter from the wind and freezing moisture. Keep yourself shielded from the wind as much as you can because that's the deadliest thing for you right now.

Now, when you're securely in place in your little igloo, you have already dialed 112 to let the rescue squad know where you are, your job is to stay awake and alive until you see lights or hear something like a truck or a snowmobile. Keeping your core temp up is essential in these situations so eat that bar of chocolate and drink the water to keep hydrated (that helps you keep warm as well). If you don't have water or you're running out of water, don't eat the snow. Try to melt it first, like against your skin for example. Consuming cold snow will cool you down faster.

Focus on your breathing, draw deep in through your nose and slowly out through your mouth. Do NOT fall asleep and monitor the progress of your shivering, letting 112 know your status regularly (if you have enough battery on your phone to stay on the line). It may be time to worry if you stop shivering. To keep warmer for longer, try to keep your limbs as close to the middle of your body as you can, if you can draw your legs under your sweater or coat, that's best. If you're not alone, use each other to keep warm.

It is possible and even probable that there is no phone service where you are. Still, the tour guide will call for help and the rescue people will try to locate your phone. So, keep it on if you can and to make things easier for them turn the location services on too. If you're all alone and you didn't let anyone know where you went, try to wait out the weather until it gets clear. Find some sort of stick to use and very carefully poke your way down the glacier and off the ice. Whatever you do, don't fall into those crevasses. If you do fall in, use any means possible to get out. They tend to close up again because the glacier is constantly on the move. Slow and deliberate is the name of the game in these situations.

You're driving along The Ring Road, minding your own business, and all of a sudden, a completely blinding snow blizzard hits. What do you do?

If you're still not stuck in a snowbank, try to keep going if you can still make out the road in front of you even if you can't see very far. In other words, if you see the sticks on the side of the road and you feel like you still have control of the vehicle, carefully continue on. If you only see one stick at a time, you're still OK to keep moving. Just drive very slowly and put your fog lights on in case there's a car coming up behind you going faster than you. It's the good old AA philosophy that counts here except it's one stick at a time instead of one day at a time. Once you're sure you're in your lane, watch the stick to your right and slowly move from stick to stick. If you stop seeing the sticks, like if the gusts blow so much snow in front of your windshield that you can't see anything, stop right away and wait until it passes. Then keep going. It only takes a second to go off the road shoulder when this happens, the blowing snow outside the window can be very disorienting.

Back in the day, when I was still a young and inexperienced driver, I got caught in a blizzard like this. Back then there were no cellphones of course, and no one knew where I was at the time and/or they thought I was at home. So, I had no choice but to keep going since I could. This was a blizzard of the extreme snow blinding variety, where everything around you is completely white. The wind outside was howling, slamming into the driver's side of the car in strong gusts and there was very slippery ice on the road and the snow just blew over it, so the ass of the car kept sliding to the right (this was also the reason I never got stuck in a bank). I was only 10 or 20 km away from home when it hit but it still took me two hours to get there. But I did it, using that AA philosophy of one stick at a time and waiting out the gusts one wind gust at a time. So it can be done but it's a scary thing to experience, especially when you're alone and no one knows where you are.

But none of this will happen to you, dear reader, since there are websites to check before going anywhere in the winter time nowadays. And if those websites predict storms and they clash with your plans, change your plans instead of taking a chance with your life and possibly other people's lives.

Photos illustrating the beauty and harshness of Icelandic nature

All pictures in this guide are by an Icelandic artist who specializes in photographing the northern lights and various bird species, although all his pictures are exquisite. His name is Þórir NK and you can see more of his work online here.

Northern Lights or Aurora Borealis as seen in September 2018 above South Iceland.

As a contrast, here is a picture taken in 2011, in the middle of the day in Vík, South Iceland, during quite a bit of ashfall. This ashfall was from the eruption in Grímsvötn, Vatnajökull glacier. It's eerie seeing the sun trying to break out of the ash cloud.

The Raven is always majestic to look at. It was just recently I found out that ravens are actually a type of passerine, but I have always heard they are very intelligent.

The ash cloud above Eyjafjallajökull glacier, heading South-East or East with the wind. Eyjafjallajökull eruption in 2010, the very same that closed down many European airports.

Mýrdalsjökull glacier in the distance with surrounding mountains and valleys, North of Vík.

An icefall connected to Mýrdalsjökull glacier, called "Kötlujökull". This kind of scenery is something you don't see very often.

The burial ground at the top of Hjörleifshöfði where it's said Hjörleifur, the second settler of Iceland is buried. Most people think he may be buried somewhere inside the rock mound on the right in the picture. The other graves are newer, they are the graves of the people who were farmers on the mountain (see picture of the farm ruins on the next page).

The ruins half-way up Hjörleifshöfði, where farmers used to live in small cabins made of dirt, grass and stone. Notice the rocky slope, left of the ruins in the photo. That's where the little track is, where you can climb up. This track is called "Lásastígur".

Waves crashing against the rocks on Reynisfjara Beach in South Iceland. This beach is one of the dangerous ones because the waves are so sneaky and appear out of nowhere. Even on days like this one.

This is what a typical Icelandic sheep with its lamb looks like. There are a lot of them roaming free around the island in the summer time, mostly up in the mountains in the middle of summer though. Icelandic sheep farmers are usually very busy helping the sheep deliver all the lambs in April/May. Not long thereafter, when the lambs are strong enough, they are let out of the fence. And off they go to enjoy the summer in the mountains, until fall.

The birdlife in Iceland is very diverse and pleasurable to watch. Here is the puffin, a long time native of Vík in the summer time. Puffins can also be seen in the Westman Islands and other places around Iceland. What I find amazing about them is that you can almost set the clock by their arrival in the spring. On April 15th to the 20th it never fails that they start pouring in, trying to find cosy and dark holes to lay their eggs.

This heart-shaped lake is so beautiful that it's almost a shame how well hidden it is between all those mountains and valleys. The name of it is Gæsavatn and it's located just south of Mýrdalsjökull glacier.

Useful links and phone numbers

The national weather channel provides current and historical information about weather forecasts, weather patterns, climate change, flooding, avalanches, earthquakes and eruptions:

https://en.vedur.is

The Department of Civil Protection and Emergency Management in Iceland:

https://www.almannavarnir.is/english

The National Road Authority provides up-to-date information about road conditions, accidents and construction on this website. Click on the map of Iceland to see conditions and click around to see different information like road humidity, wind gusts, live webcams, traffic numbers etc.:

http://www.road.is

There aren't many Icelandic news sites in English but this one is decent and seems to have relatively up-to-date information:

https://icelandmonitor.mbl.is/news

These two have the public national phone book with phone numbers, addresses and maps:
https://1819.is and https://ja.is

The national search and rescue team[25]:

http://www.icesar.com

This site is a mix of news articles in English and cultural/artistic events coming up:

https://grapevine.is

A site with all sorts of tourist information about Reykjavík:

---

[25] Note that there are regional rescue squads located around the island so only call 112 in case of an emergency.

https://visitreykjavik.is

Car rental with excellent service and decent pricing:

https://www.holdur.is/en

Public transportation routes and relevant information:

https://www.straeto.is/en

In case you run into someone who doesn't speak English this app may help:

https://play.google.com/store/apps/details?id=alldictdict.alldict.isen

If there is an emergency like an eruption in progress, the Icelandic Red Cross might have some information on where the next emergency shelter is located:

https://www.raudikrossinn.is/english

If you don't have a smart phone with mobile data and therefore might be caught in a situation where you can't go online anywhere, here are some useful phone numbers:

In case of an emergency or an accident, dial 112. This is the equivalent to 911 in The United States.

If you're going through a domestic violence situation but want advice/support before calling the police, dial 5611205.

If you have been sexually assaulted but want advice/support before calling the police, dial 8006868.

If you need a tow truck and can't call your car rental for whatever reason, dial 5676700.

If you need information about road conditions, dial 1777.

If you need information about a phone number or an address of an Icelandic resident or a business, dial 1819.

If you locked your car keys in the car (and you're in the Reykjavík area), dial 5108888..

Bibliography

Hall, Edward T. (1989). *Beyond Culture.* New York: Anchor Books - A Division of Random House, Inc.

Kjartansdóttir, Halla. (1995). *Myndir og minningar. Frásögur eftir Kjartan Leif Markússon.* Reykjavík: Halla Kjartansdóttir.

Ríkislögreglustjórinn og Almannavarnardeild. (2018). *Almannavá og áhætta.* Sótt árið 2018 af: https://www.almannavarnir.is/natturuva .

Vegagerðin. (2018). *Umferðarmerki.* Sótt árið 2018 af: http://www.vegagerdin.is/vegakerfid/umferdarmerki.

Pictures

All pictures in this guide are by Þórir N. Kjartansson, Vík, Iceland.
Format: .jpg.
Downloaded and used in this guide with author's permission: October 7th, 2018.